PAPER PLANES

DAVID MITCHELL

PAPER PLANES

25 SUPERDYNAMIC AEROPLANES TO MAKE AND FLY

COLLINS & BROWN

First published in the United Kingdom in 2017 by
Collins & Brown
43 Great Ormond Street
London
WC1N 3HZ

An imprint of Pavilion Books Company Ltd

ISBN 978-1-91116-331-2

A CIP catalogue record for this book is available from
the British Library.

10 9 8 7 6 5 4 3 2 1

Reproduction by Mission Productions Ltd, Hong Kong
Printed and bound by Leo Paper Products Ltd, China

This book can be ordered direct from the publisher at
www.pavilionbooks.com

Contents

Introduction

Paper plane design is a form of play origami, but one that has become much more a part of modern culture than mainstream origami itself. Given a piece of paper almost anyone in the world could fold the type of paper dart that every schoolchild learns, but the paper dart is just the beginning of paper plane design. There are hundreds of other designs for planes that fly faster, glide better, or perform amazing tricks and stunts that are far less well known. This book explains how to fold and fly 25 of the best – the very best.

Some of the designs are included because they are classics that are impossible to leave out. Others have been chosen because they are fun to fold or are launched in unusual ways. Check out Strike Aircraft, The Flying Pig, and Stacked Over Logan, for instance, and try them for yourself. Yet others have been chosen simply because they are different—they break the mould or bend the rules.

A paper plane is not just a paper plane. Paper planes can be designed for distance, time aloft, accuracy, stunt flying, or simply just for fun. This book contains outstanding examples of paper planes in all these categories. What's more, with the single exception of Supersonic, all the paper planes in this book are pure origami designs, meaning they are created just by folding paper, without using cuts, glue, or sticky tape.

Paper planes fly in an entirely different way to real aircraft, which have engines to provide continuous thrust and curved wings to provide lift. Paper planes have no engines: the only thrust they get comes from the way they are launched. In addition, the wings of paper planes are flat, not curved, and do not provide any lift at all. Strictly speaking, therefore, paper planes do not actually fly, they simply glide.

The flight path of a paper plane depends on the effects of five inter-related factors: launch height, initial thrust, gravity, stability, and drag.

The advantage of extra launch height is obvious. Given the same air conditions (wind is usually fatal to paper planes because it upsets their stability), the higher a plane is launched the farther it can glide.

The effect of initial thrust is much less obvious. You might imagine that the faster a plane is launched the farther it can fly, but this is not necessarily so. A good slow-launch glider will often outfly a fast-launch dart.

Gravity affects a paper plane in two ways. It pulls it back to earth, but it also provides additional energy during the flight. The wings of a paper plane are largely there to resist the downward pull of gravity, but they also allow the plane to take advantage of the additional energy on offer. You can do a simple experiment to demonstrate this. Take two sheets of paper. Screw one into a ball and keep the other flat. Drop them both. The ball drops quickly. The flat sheet has more air resistance and falls more slowly. It also flies sideways rather than just dropping straight down.

Stability is important too. A flat sheet of paper has very little. When it is dropped there is no knowing which direction it will take or what the flight characteristics will be. A good paper plane, on the other hand, has a high degree of stability. It flies in the correct attitude (the way it sits on the air) in the intended direction. The attitude of a paper plane is determined by the distribution of weight within the design. The weight of a paper plane is normally concentrated towards the front and in the keel, away from the wings. A paper plane that is tail-heavy will stall and fall. Attitude is also affected by the flight profile (the angles between the wings, keel, and other stabilizers). Normally the keel hangs down underneath the wings and acts as a weight to balance the effect of air resistance on the wings. The dihedral (the angle at which the wings are set to each other) is also important. The folding instructions for each design in this book contain a flight profile to help you set these angles correctly. The keel of a paper plane also acts as a stabilizer, which prevents the plane curving off course. A deep keel, of course, does this better than a shallow one. Additional stabilizers are often created at the wing-tips or elsewhere.

Drag is the resistance to forward movement. It acts as a brake and slows a paper plane down, and if a paper plane slows down sufficiently, it stalls. For that reason most paper planes are designed for minimum drag, which is why they are barely visible when viewed from directly in front of the nose. There are ways, however, in which drag can be employed to advantage. For example, drag can be increased by the creation of elevators at the trailing edges of the wings. This pushes the tail down and raises the nose. Elevators can often be used to improve the flight characteristics of darts and gliders, but they must be employed in a subtle way. The situation with most stunt planes is different, as they need elevators like a real plane needs aviation fuel.

The way you design and trim a paper plane depends on what you want it to do. Darts have narrow wings and are intended to fly fast and accurately in the direction they are launched. They are fairly unsubtle designs and so need very little in the way of trimming. You may occasionally find it helps to curl the tips of the trailing edges of the wings slightly upward (to provide elevators and create drag). This can sometimes ruin rather than enhance the flight characteristics, so only do it if you have to. It is much more important to fold the paper cleanly and keep all the surfaces as flat and wrinkle free as possible.

Gliders have much broader wings and are intended to fly relatively slowly. Because of this their most important flight characteristic is the glide angle. A good glider will have a glide angle that is as shallow as possible. This is achieved by organizing the folds so that the weight is distributed in a balanced way. If the natural glide angle is not shallow enough you can add elevators to improve it. Elevators however create drag and act as brakes. There is a fine line between trimming a glider too little and trimming too much.

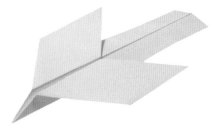

Understanding the folding instructions

The folding instructions in this book have been drawn using standard origami symbols. Most of these are self-explanatory, or consult the Dictionary of Symbols on page 127. The most important things to remember about following origami folding instructions are:

- Origami folding instructions are a sequence of separate folds that need to be followed in the correct order. Each picture in the sequence is numbered.

- Every illustration in this book is accompanied by a written instruction. Sometimes the text contains information that isn't demonstrated by the picture alone. To ensure you make the fold accurately, read the instruction beneath the picture first.

- Before you make a fold, look at the next picture to find out what the result should look like. Ignore the folding symbols for the next fold until you are ready.

- Once you understand how a fold should be made you can pick the paper up or turn it round so that you make it in the way you find easiest for you. Always remember to align your plane to the next picture and check you have got it right before moving on.

Take your time making the projects. Don't rush it. Paper planes fly better if they are made carefully.

The Paper Dart

The Paper Dart is the classic paper plane that almost every schoolchild learns in the playground. You can make one in seconds from a rectangle of almost any kind of paper. If you are one of the few who have never folded a Paper Dart before then this is your chance!

   The Paper Dart has a deep keel and narrow wings, and if launched slightly upwards at high speed it is capable of flying a long way. Its outstanding flight characteristic, however, is undoubtedly its accuracy, as many a schoolteacher has no doubt learned to their cost.

   When you have completed your dart you need to try it out. Choose a suitable target, preferably one that is not easily damaged, like a postcard pinned to a corkboard, perhaps. Try and see how often can you hit your chosen target or how far away can you hit it from.

Begin with your paper arranged in the
way shown in step 1.

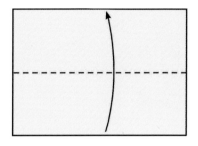

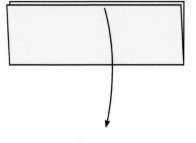

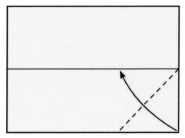

1. Fold in half upward.

2. Open out the fold made in step 1.

3. Fold the bottom right-hand corner inward using the horizontal centre crease as a guide.

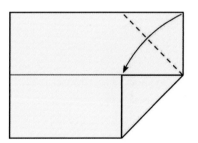

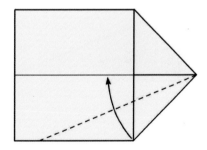

4. Fold the top right-hand corner inward in a similar way.

5. Fold the bottom right-hand corner inward so that the sloping edge lies along the vertical centre crease.

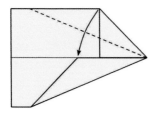

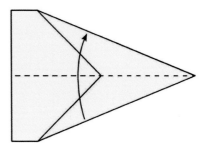

6. Fold the top right-hand corner inward in a similar way.

7. Fold in half upward.

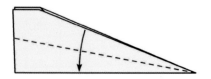

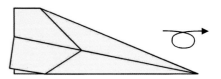

8. Form the first wing by folding just the front layers in half downward.

9. Turn over sideways.

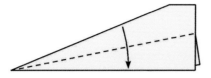

10. Form the second wing by folding the remaining layers in half downward in a similar way.

11. To prepare your dart for flight, lift the wings upward to match the profile shown.

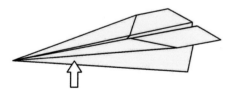

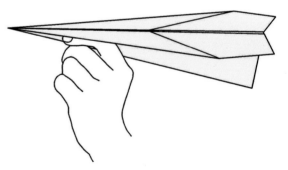

12. The Paper Dart is finished.

13. Take hold of the front of the keel between finger and thumb and launch smoothly and evenly in a slightly upward direction. Experiment with different launch speeds and angles to see what works best.

Basic Glider

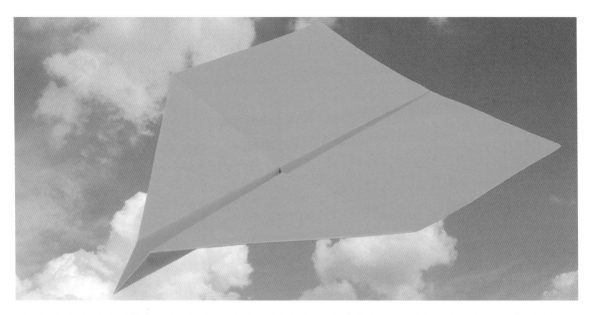

The Basic Glider is just that – a basic glider, designed to be launched at slow speed for a long, lazy gliding flight. If correctly trimmed and launched it will stay in the air for a very long time. If you can persuade it to fly in a straight line it will also fly a very long way. You will need a rectangle of ordinary paper.

If you want to understand how paper planes work, and why they fly in such very different ways, it is worth comparing the design of the Basic Glider with the design of the Paper Dart. Where the Paper Dart has a deep keel, the keel of the Basic Glider is shallow. Where the wings of the Paper Dart are narrow, the wings of the Basic Glider are large and wide. The Paper Dart is long and thin. The Basic Glider is short and broad. The result of all this is that the Paper Dart cuts through the air like a knife, while the Basic Glider floats gently to its destination as if it is resting lightly on a cushion of air.

You can experiment with different launch speeds and angles with your Basic Glider. Which combination gives the longest possible flight?

Begin with your paper arranged in
the way shown in step 1.

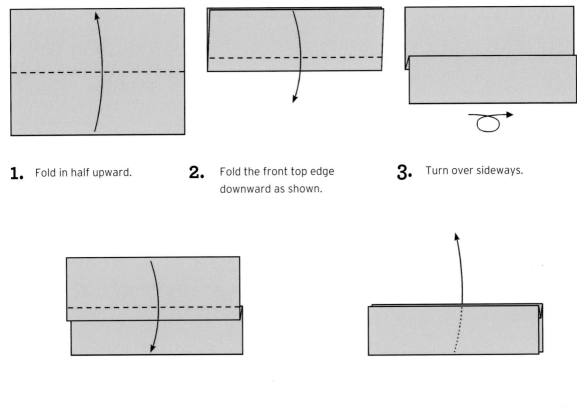

1. Fold in half upward.

2. Fold the front top edge
downward as shown.

3. Turn over sideways.

4. Fold the new front top edge downward to
match.

5. Open out the folds made in steps 1, 2, and 4 by
pulling the paper out and upward from behind.

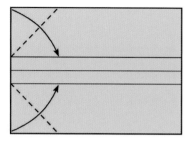 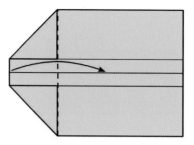 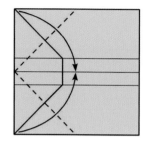

6. Fold both the left-hand corners inward using the creases made in steps 2 and 3 as guides.

7. Fold the left-hand edge inward, making sure the crease is tight to the right-hand edges of the triangular flaps.

8. Fold both left-hand corners inward again but this time using the crease made in step 1 as a guide.

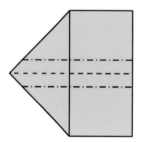

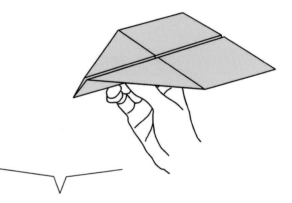

9. The shape of the glider should resemble this picture.

10. Remake the keel and wing creases through all the layers and adjust the angle of the wings to match the profile shown. Launch at medium speed for a long, gliding flight.

Strike Aircraft

Designed by David Mitchell

The *Guinness Book of Records* allows competitors the use of a small strip of sticky tape to improve the flight characteristics of their designs for its paper plane distance and time aloft records. This tape is usually used to seal the keel, which can improve the performance of the plane quite dramatically.

Strike Aircraft is an adaptation of the classic Paper Dart design in which the front of the keel is sealed without tape, just by making a few extra folds (see steps 10 through 12). You will need a rectangle of ordinary paper to make it. Launched in the normal way, Strike Aircraft is a fine fast-launch glider, but sealing the keel in this way also creates two pockets which you can use to launch Strike Aircraft in an entirely different and totally unique way. If you tuck two fingers inside the two pockets you can launch the design like a ten-pin bowling ball (except perhaps for the spin). All you need now are some skittles. (Don't forget to fold a spare!) Experiment with different launch speeds and angles. Which combination gives the longest possible flight?

Begin with your paper arranged in
the way shown in step 1.

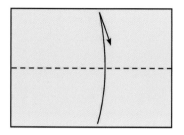

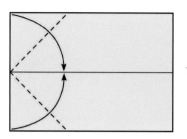

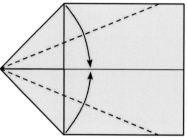

1. Fold in half upward, crease,
then unfold.

2. Fold both left-hand corners
inward using the horizontal
centre crease as a guide.

3. Thin the nose by folding
both sloping edges inward
using the horizontal crease
as a guide.

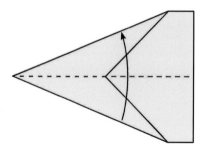

4. Fold in half from bottom to top.

5. Fold the front layer down in front to create the
left-hand wing.

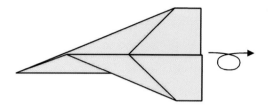

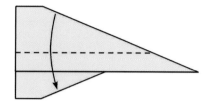

6. Turn over sideways.

7. Create the right-hand wing in a similar way, making sure all the edges of both wings line up.

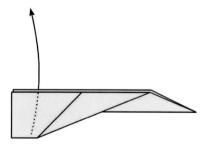

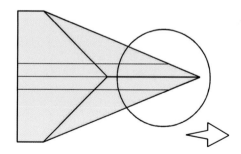

8. Open out the folds made in steps 5 and 7 by pulling the paper out upward from behind.

9. Seal the keel by following the instructions in the enlargements.

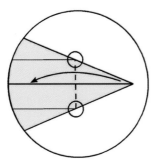

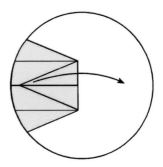

10. First fold the tip of the nose inward. The new crease should run between the ends of the two creases separating the wings from the keel.

11. Open out the fold made in step 10.

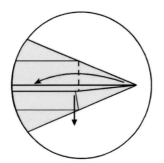

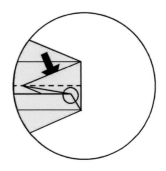

12. Open out the bottom half of the top layers of the nose and refold the tip of the nose inward underneath them.

13. You have created a flap (marked with a circle) and a pocket (shown by the arrow). Tuck the flap inside the pocket to reform the nose. This is difficult but not quite impossible!

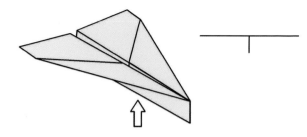 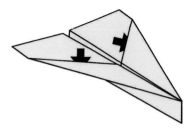

14. Remake the keel and wing creases and adjust the angle of the wings to match the profile shown. The result will be a blunt-nosed glider that looks like this. Launched in the conventional way this glider will fly well. Because of the blunt nose it can be launched at high speed.

15. You can also launch this plane in a completely unconventional way. There are two pockets underneath the flaps on top of the wings.

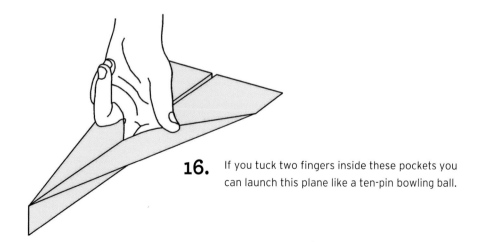

16. If you tuck two fingers inside these pockets you can launch this plane like a ten-pin bowling ball.

The Rapier

The Rapier is what you might get if you crossed the Paper Dart with the Basic Glider. A simple tuck (made in steps 8 and 9) shortens and rebalances the entire design and gives it a sharp pointed nose, like a rapier, and wide, stubby wings. The result is a plane that can be launched fast or slow, or somewhere in between.

A rectangle of ordinary paper is all you will need. Bear in mind that the point of the Rapier is hard and sharp (at least until the first time you fly it into a wall at speed) and take care that you are not throwing it in the direction of innocent bystanders.

You could make a Paper Dart, a Basic Glider, and a Rapier from three identical sheets of paper. Find out which one flies farthest. Which one stays in the air for the longest time? Which design looks best?

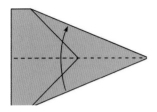

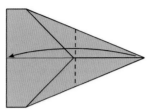

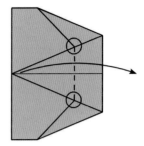

Begin by following steps 1 through 7 of the Paper Dart (page 10) so that your paper looks like this.

8. Fold in half from right to left.

9. Fold the tip of the nose out to the right again. The circles show you how to locate this fold.

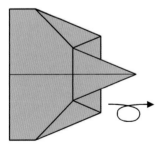

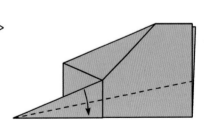

10. Turn over sideways.

11. Fold in half upward. The next picture is on a larger scale.

12. Fold the top layer of the nose in half downward. Extend this crease all the way to the right edge of the paper.

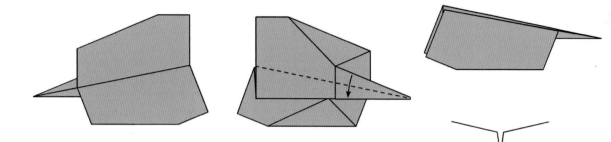

13. Turn over sideways.

14. Fold the other wing downward to match in a similar way.

15. Lift the wings upward to match the profile shown.

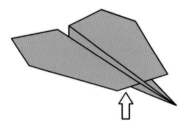

16. Hold the Rapier at the point shown and launch fast.

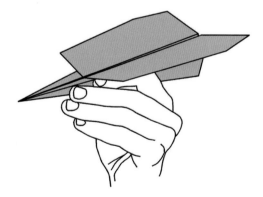

17. The Rapier will travel a surprisingly long distance if you throw it hard enough. Bear this in mind if you are throwing in the direction of innocent bystanders. The point of the Rapier is hard and sharp.

The Norton Flyer

Some paper planes are a joy to fold. Some fly extremely well. The Norton Flyer combines the two, and is undoubtedly one of the best paper planes ever designed. You will need a rectangle of ordinary paper.

The secret of the design is that the exact centre of the paper (steps 1 and 2) is used to locate the next five folds that create the overall shape and balance of the design. After that all you need to do is make two equally well-located folds to create the keel and the wings.

Since all the folds are located exactly (which means all the planes should be virtually identical to each other), this design makes an excellent choice for a paper plane contest designed to test the piloting skills of the contestants.

Like many other simple planes, the Norton Flyer flies best if the dihedral (the angle between the wings) is slightly less than 180 degrees (see the flight profile in step 14). Try making subtle changes to the profile to see if you can improve (or worsen) the flight characteristics of this design.

Begin with your paper arranged in the way shown in step 1.

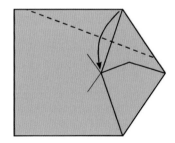

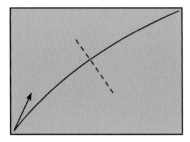

1. Fold in half diagonally, make a small crease in the centre (not right the way across), then unfold.

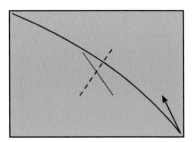

2. Fold in half from right to left.

3. The point where the creases cross is the centre of the paper. This point is used to locate the next five folds. It is easier to see the creases if you turn the paper over sideways now.

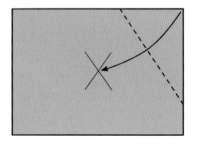

4. Fold the top right-hand corner onto the centre point.

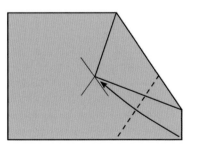

5. Fold the bottom right-hand corner onto the centre point in a similar way.

6. Fold the new top right-hand corner onto the centre point. Do this as accurately as you can.

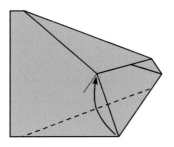 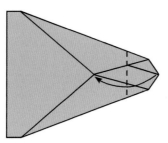 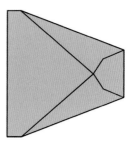

7. Fold the new bottom right-hand corner onto the centre point in a similar way.

8. Fold the tip of the nose onto the centre point as well.

9. Turn over sideways.

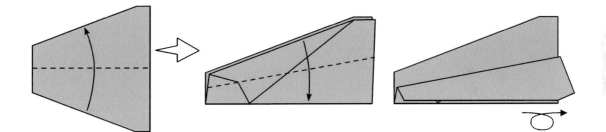

10. Fold in half upward. The next picture is on a larger scale.

11. Fold the front wing in half downward.

12. Turn over sideways.

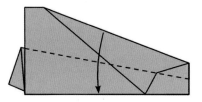

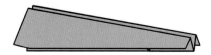

13. Fold the second wing in half downward in a similar way.

14. Lift the wings upward and loosen the folds of the keel to match the profile shown.

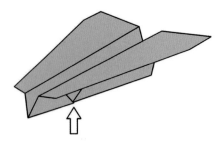

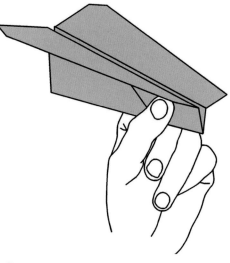

15. The Norton Flyer is finished.

16. Pinch the keel together to launch in the normal way.

Thunderbolt

All the other planes in this book are made from just a single piece of paper, but Thunderbolt is made from two. One piece is used to create the nose and the wings and the other the tail. Both pieces can easily be cut from a single rectangle. The folds that form the wings also lock the two pieces of paper firmly together.

   The result is Thunderbolt, a paper plane shaped like an avenging arrow, that will fly as fast as lightning. Truly the paper plane of the gods.

   Try launching Thunderbolt from the Olympian height of a second floor window (or higher). Pick yourself a target. How accurate can you be? Remember that inanimate targets are slower-moving and easier to hit. You also stand a better chance of being able to recover your Thunderbolt undamaged afterward.

Begin with your paper arranged in the
way shown in step 1.

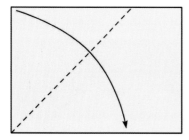 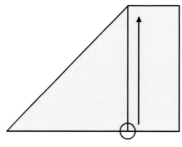 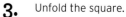 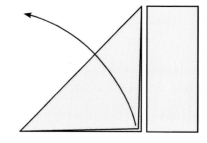

1. Fold the left-hand edge onto
the bottom edge. Hold the
edges together and crease
firmly.

2. Hold the sheets firmly
together and in alignment,
especially at the point
marked with a circle, and
cut carefully along the
upright edge, working
from bottom to top.

3. Unfold the square.

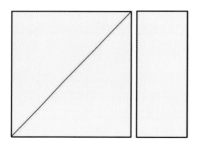

Folding the tail: The tail is made from the
smaller rectangle.

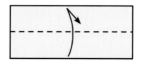

4. Both pieces of paper are needed for Thunderbolt.

5. Fold in half from bottom to top, crease,
then unfold.

 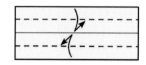 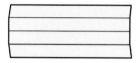

6. Turn over sideways.

7. Fold both long edges inward to lie along the crease made in step 5, crease, then unfold but don't flatten the creases.

8. The tail is finished.

Folding the wings:
The wings are made from the square.

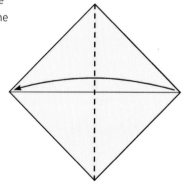 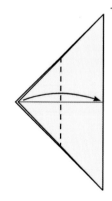

9. Fold in half from right to left.

10. Fold the left-hand point across to the right. Make this fold in all the layers.

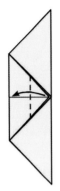 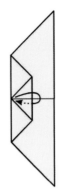 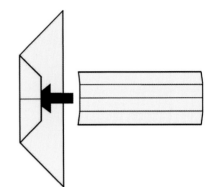

11. Fold the top two layers back across to the left.

12. (Optional) Swing the top flaps (both layers) out of sight by reversing the direction of the crease made in step 11.

13. Slide the tail inside the nose. Make sure the tail is arranged so that the edges are turned slightly backward (i.e. turned over from the position shown in step 8).

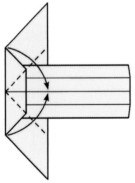 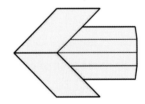

14. Fold the left-hand edge of both wings inward to lie along the central horizontal crease. This will lock the two sheets of paper together.

15. This is the result. The two parts of the plane are now locked together.

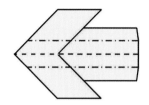

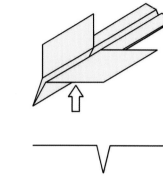

16. Remake the creases formed in the tail in steps 5 and 7 through all the layers of the nose and wings. Crease very firmly.

17. Arrange the wings and tail to match the profile shown.

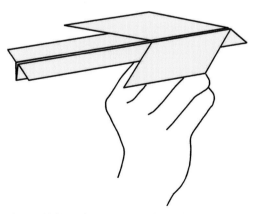

18. Hold the keel underneath the wings and launch at high speed. You will be able to launch Thunderbolt using all your strength. In the right weather conditions it will fly a long way.

Max's Stunt Plane

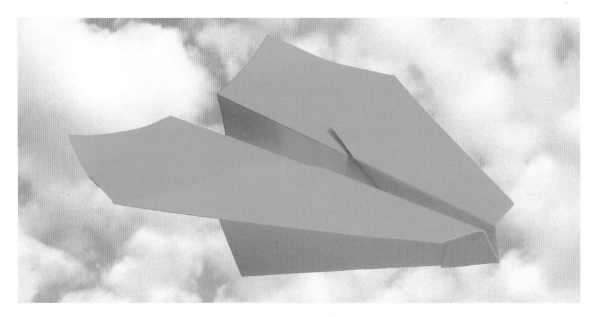

Stunt planes are designed to fly in loops and circles. It is very difficult to persuade a paper plane to fly more than one loop (you simply can't launch it fast enough) but you should be able to achieve several circles if you launch a well-trimmed stunt plane from a decent height in still air, even perhaps in your own living room.

Max's Stunt Plane has been around (and around and around) long enough to be considered a classic by paper plane aficionados but it is still hard to find a design that will outperform it.

You can launch Max's Stunt Plane in almost any way you choose. To the left, to the right, upward, backward over your shoulder, almost any way at all except straight down, in fact.

You will need a square of ordinary paper. Steps 1 through 3 of Thunderbolt show you how to cut a square from a rectangle. When you have completed the plane, stand with it beside a chair. Try to launch Max's Stunt Plane so that it circles around to land gently on the chair. Difficult, yes, but quite possible with practice.

Begin with your paper arranged in the
way shown in step 1.

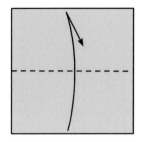

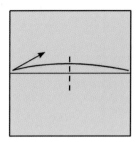

1. Fold in half from bottom to top,
crease, then unfold.

2. Fold in half from right to left, make a small
crease to mark the half-way point, then unfold.

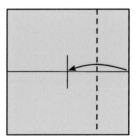

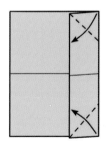

3. Fold the right hand edge inward using the
small crease made in step 2 as a guide.

4. Fold both corners of the rectangular
flap inward.

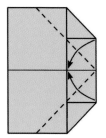 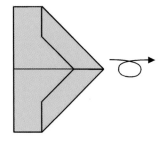 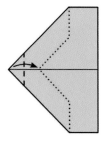

5. Fold both right-hand corners inward using the horizontal centre crease as a guide.

6. Turn over sideways.

7. Fold the tip of the nose inward like this. The dotted line shows the edges of the hidden layers.

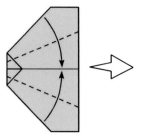 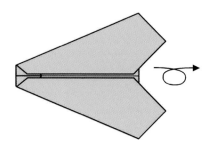

8. Fold both sloping edges inward using the horizontal crease as a guide. The next picture is on a larger scale.

9. Turn over sideways.

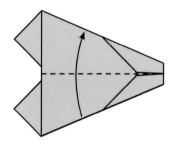

10. Fold in half upward.

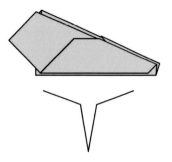

11. Raise the wings to match the profile shown.

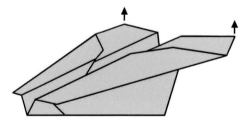

12. Curl the tips of the wings upward.

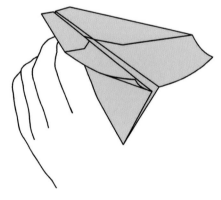

13. Hold just behind the turned-back part of the nose and launch at medium speed.

The Whirling Wing

The Whirling Wing is not a paper plane, but it is made of paper and it certainly does fly, if not in an entirely orthodox way.

The Whirling Wing is just a simple strip of paper. If you hold it high in the air between finger and thumb in the way shown in step 7 and give the back edge a very slight downward flick as you release it, the Whirling Wing will begin to whirl around its longer axis. It will carry on whirling and fly a gentle spiral until it hits the ground. Why it behaves in this strange way is something of a mystery.

You can make the Whirling Wing fly in a straight line by adding wing-tip stabilisers in the way shown in step 8. Wing-tip stabilisers can also be added to many standard paper plane designs (like the Basic Glider, perhaps?) to constrain them to a straighter, more stable flight path. You can experiment further with this by making Whirling Wings from longer or wider strips, or try giving the Whirling Wing a central keel.

Begin by following steps 1 through 3 of Thunderbolt.
The Whirling Wing is made from the smaller rectangle.

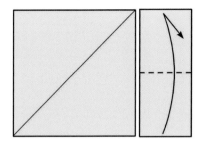 

4. Save the square for another project. Fold the long, thin rectangle in half upward, crease, then unfold.

5. Fold in half from right to left, crease, then unfold.

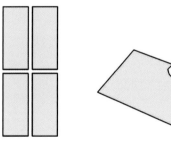

6. Cut along the creases to create four smaller rectangles of the same shape.

7. Take one of these rectangles and hold it high in the air like this. As you let it go give the back edge a slight downward flick. This is the Whirling Wing, the simplest flying object.

8. Your Whirling Wing will probably fly in a spiral. To give it a sense of direction fold both ends up at right-angles like this. Then try again.

Designed by David Mitchell

Zigzag

However you choose to view it, Zigzag is a most unusual paper plane design. It is either all keel and no wing, or all wing and no keel, whichever way you like to look at it. You can also choose to see Zigzag as a Whirling Wing that has been weighted along one edge to stop it whirling. The strange thing is that it flies at all ... but fly it does!

Another apparently odd aspect of the Zigzag design is that the plane is configured one way when it is launched, but adopts a different configuration when it is flying through the air. When it is launched it looks like step 13. When it is flying it looks like step 12. This, though, is not as unusual as it seems. Because of the effect of gravity and the resistance of the air below the wings, all paper planes fly in a slightly different configuration to the one they are launched in. Zigzag is just an extreme example.

You will need a rectangle of ordinary paper. After you have completed Zigzag you could try and see if it still flies with more (or less) zigzags in the wings, or do the zigzags on one side need to be the same as the zigzags on the other?

Begin with your paper arranged in
the way shown in step 1.

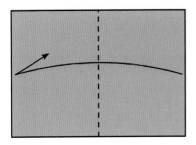

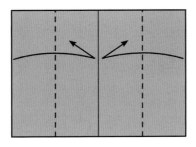

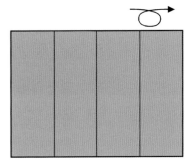

1. Fold in half from right to left,
crease, then unfold.

2. Fold both outside edges
into the centre, crease,
then unfold.

3. Turn over sideways.

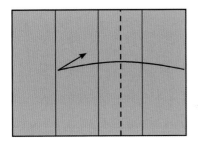

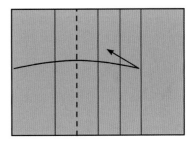

4. Fold the right-hand edge inward using the left-
hand crease as a guide, crease, then unfold.

5. Repeat the fold described in step 4 on
the left-hand edge.

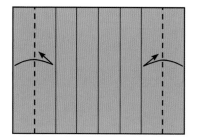

6. Fold both outside edges inward to the nearest crease line, crease, then unfold.

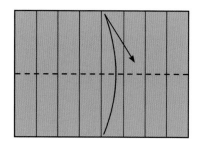

7. Fold in half from bottom to top, crease, then unfold.

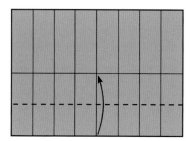

8. Fold the bottom edge upward.

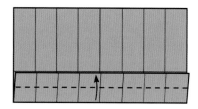

9. Fold the new bottom edge upward as well.

10. Fold the new bottom edge upward one final time using the crease made in step 7.

11. Use the creases made in steps 1 through 6 to form the paper into a zigzag wing. The result should look like step 12.

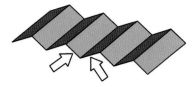

12. Zigzag is finished. The thick layers of paper are at the front.

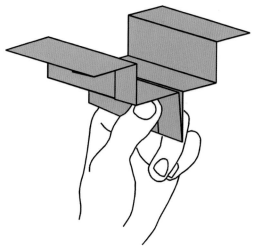

13. Launch by pinching the thick layers of the central keel together at the front. If launched fairly gently Zigzag will quickly assume its shape and will fly unexpectedly well.

Designed by David Mitchell

Cupid's Arrow

A paper plane in the shape of a heart? Surely not! You will need a rectangle of ordinary paper. Make Cupid's Arrow and test fly it until you are sure you can launch it, so that it flies reasonably well. This is not so easy. You may need to make and fly several Cupid's Arrows before you are happy that you have acquired the knack. Launching gently is important. So is curving the creases made in steps 8 and 11 so that the flaps do not stick out and create drag.

When you are confident that you will not seriously embarrass yourself in public, get all your favorite friends together at a party, line them up, and launch Cupid's Arrow gently toward them. Aim carefully by all means, but be warned, Cupid's Arrow does not always strike the one you are aiming at.

Begin with your paper arranged in the
way shown in step 1.

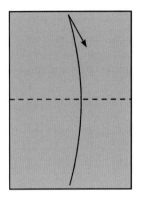

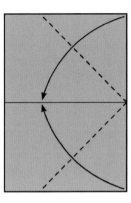

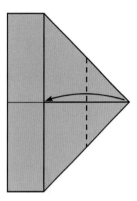

1. Fold in half upward, crease
firmly, then unfold.

2. Fold both right-hand corners
inward using the crease
made in step 1 as a guide.

3. Fold the tip of the right-
hand point inward as shown.

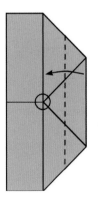

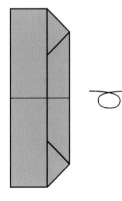

4. Fold the right-hand edge inward as shown,
making sure the point marked with a circle
doesn't move.

5. Turn over sideways.

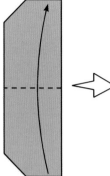 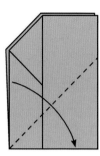 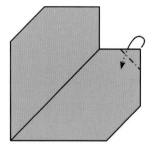

6. Fold in half upward using the crease made in step 1. The next step is on a larger scale.

7. Fold the front layers in half diagonally.

8. Fold the tip of the front layer backward as shown. Make the crease slightly convex to hold the flap in place.

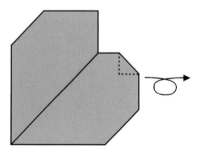 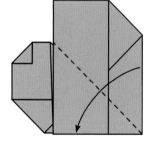

9. Turn over sideways.

10. Fold the new front flap in half diagonally as well.

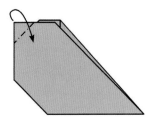

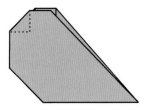

11. Fold the tip of the front wing backward to match. Make the crease slightly convex to hold the flap in place.

12. Open up the wings to match the profile shown.

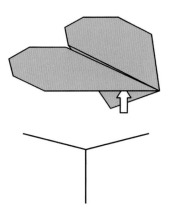

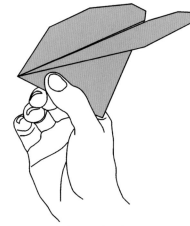

13. Cupid's Arrow is finished.

14. Launch gently in the classic manner. Be careful where you aim!

Designed by David Mitchell

The Sky Scooter

Some paper planes are destined for greatness. Others are simply destined to crash into the opposite wall. Some paper planes have an affinity for the floor and head there in the minimum distance, but Sky Scooter has an affinity for the ceiling.

Outwardly Sky Scooter is a very normal kind of paper plane made from a rectangle of ordinary paper. It has a normal sort of keel, sealed at the front, and the normal kind of wings. If you launch it in a normal kind of way, it will fly a normal sort of distance at a fairly normal speed. If, however, you curl the tips of the wings upward as if you are trying to turn it into a stunt plane (which won't work because the wings are too long) and then launch it fast along the underside of a wide ceiling (taking care to avoid obstructions like light fittings, smoke detectors or house-bats) an extraordinary thing happens. Sky Scooter clings to the ceiling all the way across the room until it crashes into the opposite wall. Why does this happen? Who knows! Some ceilings are smoother, wider, and generally much better suited to scooting than others.

Begin with your paper arranged in the way
shown in step 1.

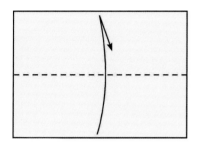

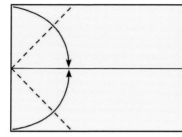

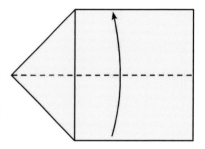

1. Fold in half upward, crease,
then unfold.

2. Fold both left-hand corners
inward using the horizontal
centre crease as a guide.

3. Fold in half upward.

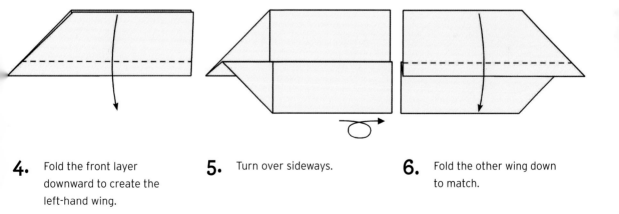

4. Fold the front layer
downward to create the
left-hand wing.

5. Turn over sideways.

6. Fold the other wing down
to match.

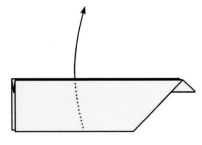

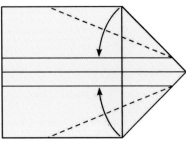

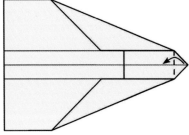

7. Open out the folds made in steps 3, 4, and 6 by pulling the paper upward from behind.

8. Narrow the wings using the creases formed in steps 4 and 5 as guides.

9. Fold the triangular tip of the nose inward.

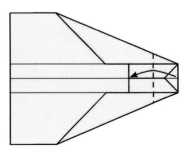

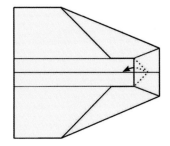

10. Fold the nose inward again so that the blunt tip of the nose lines up with the edges of the flaps created in step 2.

11. Pull out the hidden flap.

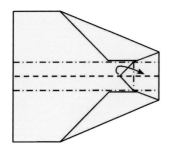

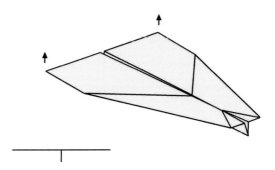

12. Reform the keel using the existing creases. As you do this the small triangular flap will fold in half. Tuck this flap away sideways behind the loose layer beside it to lock the keel together. This is difficult but by no means impossible.

13. Adjust the wings to match the profile shown, then curl the tips of the wings upward as if you are making a stunt plane.

14. The Sky Scooter is finished. The plane shown in step 13 is a perfectly good slow launch glider. By curling the tips of the wings, however, you have effectively ruined its flight characteristics, but ruined them to good purpose. If you hold the Sky Scooter close to a smooth, wide ceiling and launch it firmly along the ceiling (aiming to avoid any light fittings or smoke alarms) the Sky Scooter will scoot along the ceiling until it collides with the opposite wall. Weird, but true.

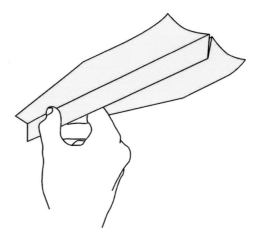

Trick Stunter

Aerobatic aircraft can fly two different kinds of loops. When flying an outside loop, the plane is the right way up at the bottom of the loop and upside down at the top. When flying an inside loop, the plane is the right way up at the top but upside down at the bottom. Paper stunt planes will generally only fly outside loops, but the Trick Stunter will fly inside loops as well. You just have to hold it in a different place when you launch it. And you have to launch it very fast.

You can use this strange characteristic to tease your friends. First demonstrate how the Trick Stunter flies outside loops in the normal way. Then get a friend to try, but tell him or her to hold the plane right at the front. Make sure they launch it with all their strength. The plane will fly an inside loop instead. Provided they always hold the Trick Stunter right at the front, they will never be able to make it stunt in the normal way.

You will need a rectangle of ordinary paper.
Begin with your paper arranged in the way
shown in step 1.

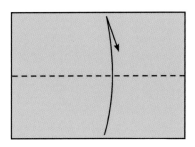

1. Fold in half upwards, crease, then unfold.

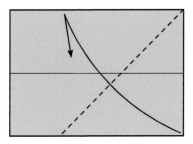

2. Fold the right-hand edge onto the top edge, crease, then unfold.

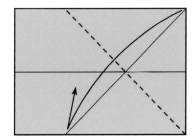

3. Fold the right-hand edge onto the bottom edge, crease, then unfold.

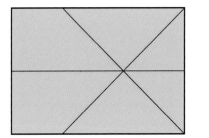

4. Turn over sideways.

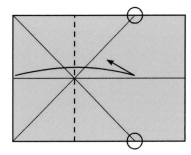

5. Fold the left-hand edge inward so that the corners touch the points where the diagonal creases intersect the top and bottom edges (marked with circles), crease, then unfold. The new crease will pass through the point where the diagonal creases made in steps 2 and 3 intersect.

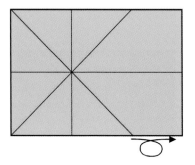 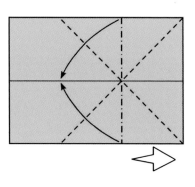 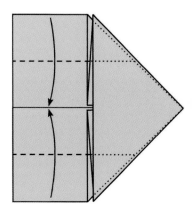

6. Turn over sideways.

7. Collapse into the form shown in step 8. Step 8 has been drawn on a larger scale.

8. Fold the top and bottom edges of the rear layers inward to lie along the horizontal crease.
Try to make sure you don't crease the front flaps as you do this.

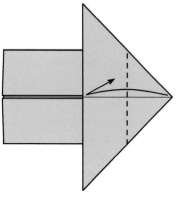 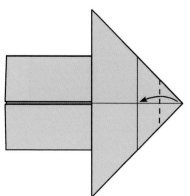

9. Fold the triangular flap in half inward, crease, then unfold.

10. Fold the tip of the triangular flap in half inward, using the crease made in step 9 as a guide.

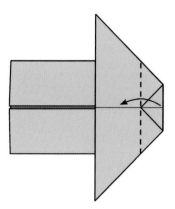 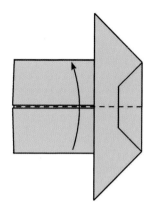 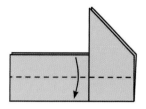

11. Fold the tip of the nose inward again, using the crease made in step 9. Crease firmly.

12. Fold in half from upwards.

13. Fold the top edge of the bottom layers onto the top edge.

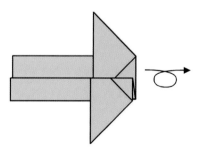 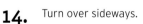 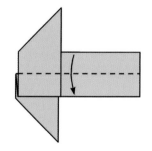

14. Turn over sideways.

15. Fold the top edge of the front layers onto the bottom edge.

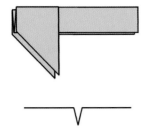

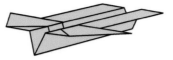

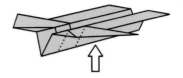

16. Lift the wings to match the profile shown.

17. The Trick Stunter must be launched at high speed. You will need all your strength to make it perform aerobatics. It will fly both outside and inside loops depending on where you hold the keel as you launch it.

18. To make your Trick Stunter fly outside loops (the kind of loops that stunt paper planes normally fly), hold the keel in the middle or slightly toward the back.

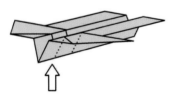

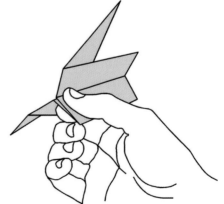

19. To make your Trick Stunter fly inside loops, hold the keel toward the front.

20. This picture shows the Trick Stunter being launched to perform an inside loop.

Michael La Fosse Design

Stacked Over Logan

This delicately delightful design is named for the aircraft stacked awaiting clearance to land over Logan International Airport near where the designer lives.

The unique feature of this design is that, because of its elegant simplicity and lack of a clearly defined keel, a number of planes can be stacked on top of each other and launched together. Because the design is not directionally stable, the stack will soon peel apart and each individual plane will take off on its own trajectory, curving and weaving downward. If you make your planes from brightly coloured origami paper the effect can be quite spectacular. Of course you can also have fun launching the planes individually.

You will need a square of paper (origami paper is ideal). Begin with your paper arranged in the way shown in step 1.

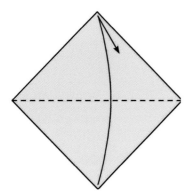

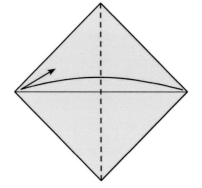

1. Fold in half upward, crease, then unfold.

2. Fold in half sideways, crease, then unfold.

3. Fold the left-hand point inward to the centre of the paper.

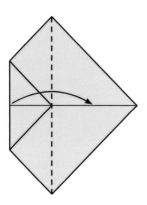

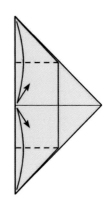

4. Fold the left-hand edge inward, using the crease made in step 2.

5. Fold the top and bottom corners inward as shown, crease, then unfold.

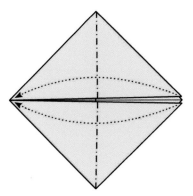

6. Fold the top and bottom corners inward to the right as shown. The next step is on a larger scale.

7. Fold both front flaps in half backward into the pockets that lie behind them using the creases made in step 5.

8. Fold the top and bottom corners inward to the centre.

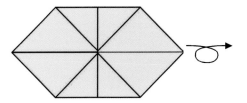

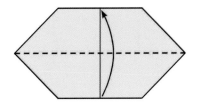

9. Turn over sideways.

10. Fold in half upward.

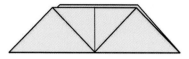

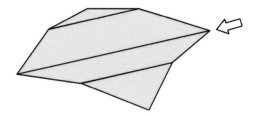

11. Open out to match the profile shown.

12. Hold at the back (where there is only a single thickness of paper) and launch with a gentle push forward.

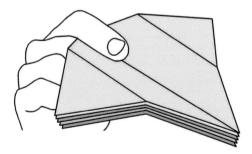

13. Because the design is so simple a number of these planes can be stacked on top of each other and launched simultaneously. They will fly away in all directions.

The Flying Pig

If you have reached this stage in the book you will already know that not all paper planes are the same. Some very strange-looking designs can take to the skies. And the name? Is it called the Flying Pig because it has wings and a definitely pig-like snout? Or simply because that's the way it flies? The Flying Pig is basically a short triangular tube equipped with stubby wings. It shouldn't really fly at all. But it does. Occasionally it even flies quite well.

It is also launched in a most unusual way. You have to hold it by the nose and pull it in the general direction you would prefer to fly, remembering to let go before it has headed for the floor. Running with it in the way you might run to launch a particularly ground-loving kite might help as well. There is a definite art to this. Get it right and the Flying Pig will glide surprisingly well. You could try the effect of curling the wing-tips slightly. Only slightly, mind. This is not by any means a Flying Stunt Pig.

You will need a rectangle of ordinary paper. Begin with your paper arranged in the way shown in step 1.

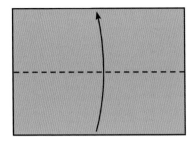

1. Fold in half upward.

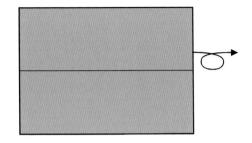

2. Turn over sideways.

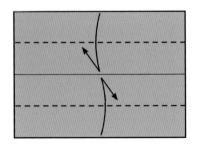

3. Fold the top and bottom edges inward using the crease made in step 1 as a guide, crease, then unfold.

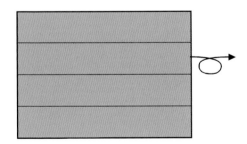

4. Turn over sideways again.

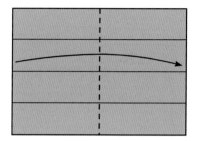

5. Fold in half from left to right.

6. Fold both left-hand corners inward, using the creases made in step 3 as guides.

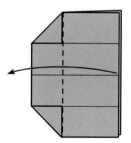

7. Fold the front right-hand edge across to the left as far as it will go.

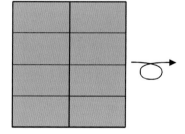

8. Turn over sideways.

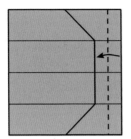

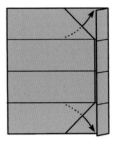

9. Fold the right-hand edge inward to lie against the vertical folded edge.

10. Pull out the hidden flaps.

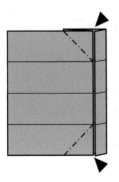

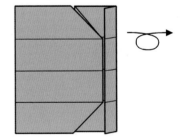

11. Turn the corners inside out between the other layers using the existing creases.

12. Turn over sideways.

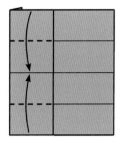

13. There are two loose flaps on the left-hand side. Fold them both inward using the existing creases.

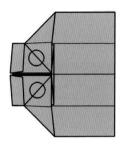

14. Raise the flaps marked with circles slightly so that your plane looks like step 15.

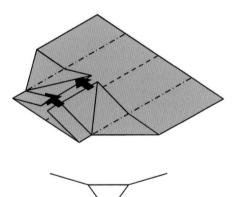

15. Push one flap inside the other (either way) and gently reform the keel and wing creases to match the profile shown.

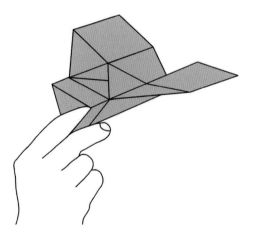

16. Hold in the way shown here and launch with a firm gliding pull. There is a definite art to this. Get it right and the Flying Pig will glide satisfyingly well.

Designed by David Mitchell

The Condor

The Condor is a fine example of a wide-wing paper plane design. Wide-wings are notoriously difficult to design. They tend to have an unnerving tendency to either dive straight to the floor or adopt the Whirling Wing flight mode. That the Condor succumbs to neither of these unfortunate fates, and flies straight and true, is probably due to the tiny triangular flaps below the wings. The flight of the Condor is unusual in one other respect: it flaps its wings in flight. You can increase or decrease the flapping action by adjusting the angle of the triangular flaps underneath the wings.

You will need a rectangle of ordinary paper. Begin with your
paper arranged in the way shown in step 1.

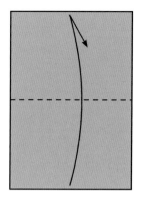

1. Fold in half upward, crease,
then unfold.

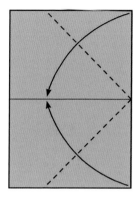

2. Fold both right-hand
corners inward using
the crease made in step 1
as a guide.

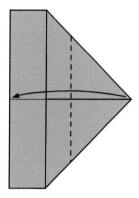

3. Fold in half from right
to left.

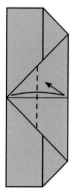

4. Fold the point of the front
flap back across to the
right-hand edge, crease,
then unfold.

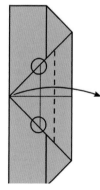

5. Fold the point of the front
flap across to the right so
that the crease made in
step 4 lies on the right-
hand edge.

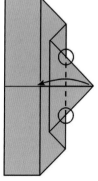

6. Fold the point back
across to the left
using the crease made
in step 4.

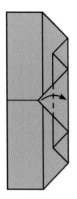 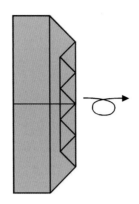 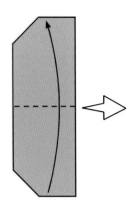

7. Fold the point back across to the right once more.

8. Turn over sideways.

9. Fold in half upward. The next picture is on a larger scale.

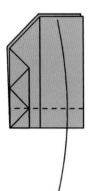 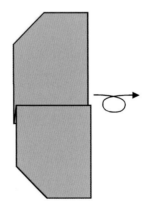 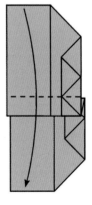

10. Fold the first wing downward using the tip of the small triangle at bottom left to locate the fold.

11. Turn over sideways.

12. Fold the second wing downward to match.

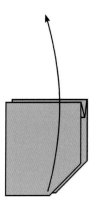

13. Open out the front wing and the keel in an upward direction.

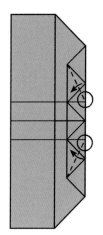

14. Make the folds made here to create two tiny triangular flaps.

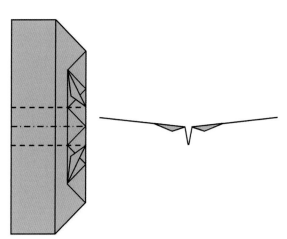

15. This is the underside of the wings. Remake the wing and keel folds and lower the triangular flaps slightly to match the profile shown.

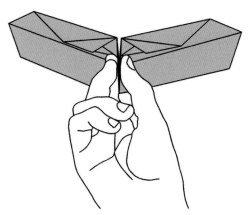

16. Hold like this and launch gently in the normal way. The wings of the Condor will oscillate during flight as if the Condor is flapping its wings. You can increase or decrease the flapping action by adjusting the angle of the triangular flaps underneath the wings.

Catch Me

Sometimes you don't need to change a design by very much to alter its flight characteristics entirely. The original design on which Catch Me is based was folded from a square. In its original form, particularly when folded from origami paper, the plane is a wonderful glider. By folding it from a rectangle of ordinary paper, which lengthens the wings and alters the weight distribution throughout the design (and by curling the wingtips) I have managed to create Catch Me. This is a paper plane that comes back to you to be caught, time and time again. There's an element of skill in this, of course. Practise standing up first, then sitting down. You will soon be able to achieve a consistent throw and catch, even in quite small spaces.

The elegant way in which the nose is locked together, sealing the keel, comes directly from the original design and is one of the most innovative design elements in the paper plane repertoire. Try flying Catch Me around a lamp-post, a pillar, or a particularly skinny friend.

You will need a rectangle of ordinary paper. Begin with your paper arranged in the way shown in step 1.

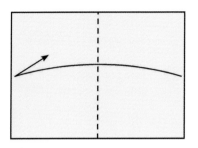

1. Fold in half sideways, crease, then unfold.

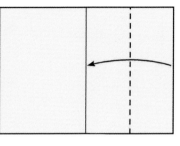

2. Fold the right-hand edge onto the vertical crease.

3. Fold in half upward, crease, then unfold.

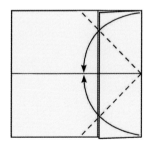

4. Fold both right-hand corners inward, using the crease made in step 3 as a guide.

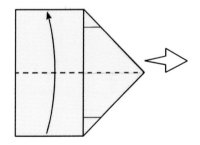

5. Fold in half upward, using the crease made in step 3. The next picture is on a larger scale.

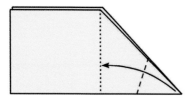 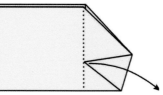 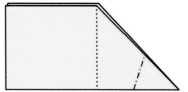

6. Fold the tip of the nose inward as far as the edge of the hidden layers. You can see where this edge is if you hold the paper up to the light. Try to make your model look as much like step 7 as possible.

7. Open out the fold made in step 6.

8. Turn the nose inside out between the other layers.

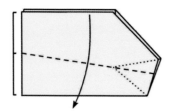 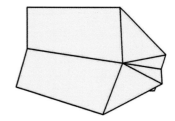

9. Form one wing by folding the top edge downward along a line that runs from halfway up the left-hand edge through the point of the layers you turned inside out in step 8. Try to be as accurate with this fold as you can.

10. Turn over sideways.

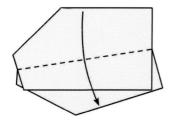

11. Fold the second wing downward to match the first.

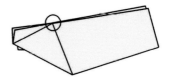

12. If you have followed the instructions correctly, the layers will be locked together at the point marked with a circle. Raise the wings.

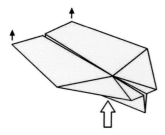

13. Curl the wingtips upward to complete the design.

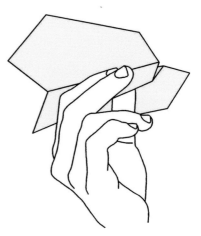

14. If you throw this amazing stunter upward and slightly outward (out to the left if you are right-handed and vice versa) you will be able to catch Catch Me when it comes gliding back to you. Practise standing up first, then sitting down.

Designed by Nick Robinson

Aerobat

Aerobat is a hybrid plane that combines the characteristics of a stunt plane and a long-distance glider. The unusual shape of the trailing edges of the wings makes it possible to provide Aerobat with both wing-tip stabilisers and elevators. The result is a plane that will stunt in the first phase of its flight then settle into a long, gentle glide. Two planes for the price of one, in fact.

Elevators are provided by curling the tip of the trailing edges of the wings upward. The tips of both wings need to be curled roughly the same amount. The effect of elevators is to create drag at the back of the plane, which forces the tail down and the nose up. If the amount of the initial thrust is enough to overcome the slowing effect of this drag, your plane will loop or circle (depending whether you launched it lying flat or at an angle). If Aerobat stalls, you have curled the wings too much. If it flies straight, you have not curled them enough. You could also try the effect of making Aerobat from lighter paper.

You will need a square of ordinary paper.
Begin with your paper arranged in the way
shown in step 1.

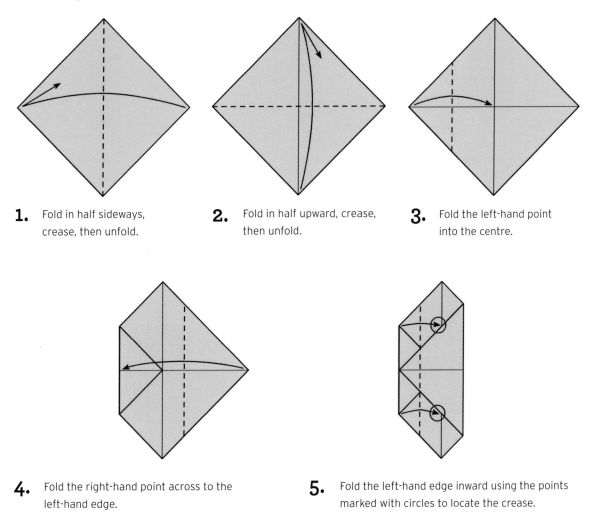

1. Fold in half sideways, crease, then unfold.

2. Fold in half upward, crease, then unfold.

3. Fold the left-hand point into the centre.

4. Fold the right-hand point across to the left-hand edge.

5. Fold the left-hand edge inward using the points marked with circles to locate the crease.

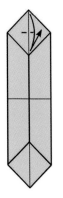 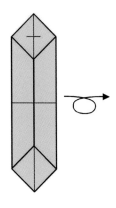 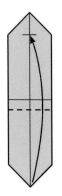

6. There is a small square area at the top of the design which is just a single layer of paper thick. Fold this square area in half downward, make a tiny crease in the centre, then unfold.

7. Turn over sideways.

8. Create the first wing by folding the bottom point upward. Use the tiny crease made in step 6 to locate this fold.

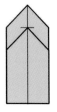 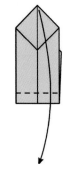

9. Turn over sideways.

10. Fold the top point downward using the crease made in step 1.

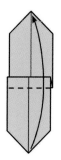

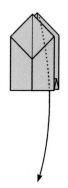

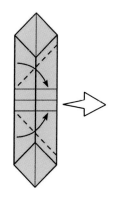

11. Fold the second wing upwards to match.

12. Open out the back wing and keel in a downward direction.

13. Fold both the top and bottom points to the right using the creases made in steps 8 and 11 as guides. The next picture is on a larger scale.

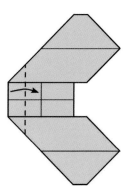

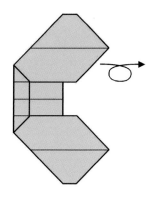

14. Fold the nose inward to create extra weight at the front and trap the wings in place.

15. Turn over sideways.

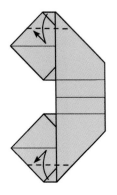

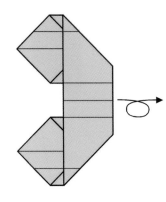

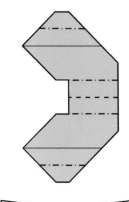

16. Fold both wingtips inward to form stabilizers, crease, then unfold.

17. Turn over sideways.

18. Remake the keel, wing and stabilizer folds to match the profile shown.

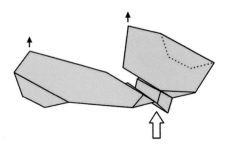

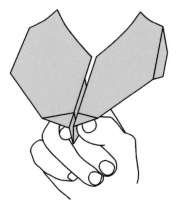

19. Curl the wingtips upward.

20. Hold at the front of the keel and launch fast in a slightly downward direction. Properly trimmed, Aerobat will swoop upward then settle into a long, gliding flight.

The Samurai

The design of the Samurai was developed from a traditional Japanese paperfold known as the Kabuto or Samurai Helmet. You can see the shape of this helmet, with its twin horns, in step 12.

At first sight the Samurai seems a very unlikely sort of paper plane. The wings are fairly normal, but all that extra clutter at the front looks as though it should prevent the plane flying well. It doesn't though, as the small extra wings at the front – known as Canard wings – seem to add a great deal of extra stability. The Samurai will glide well both ways up, with the keel below or above the wings, and the horns provide an easy way to launch the Samurai the wrong way up. Canard wings also feature in the design of Supersonic (page 103), which will also fly with the keel above the wings.

You will need a rectangle of ordinary paper. Begin by following steps 1 through 7 of the Trick Stunter (see page 52).

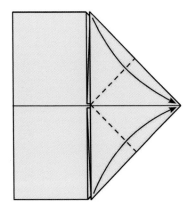

8. Fold both the front triangular flaps in half.

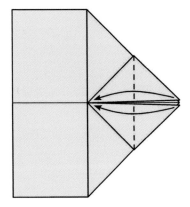

9. Fold both the new triangular flaps in half as well.

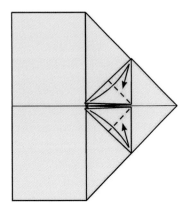

10. Fold the new triangular flaps in half again but this time crease, then unfold.

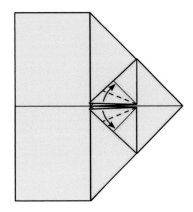

11. Fold the tips of the new triangular flaps outward, using the creases made in step 10 as a guide.

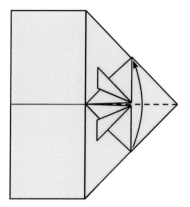

12. Fold just the front layers in half upward.

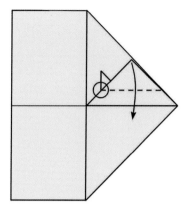

13. Fold the point of the front flap back downward. The new crease should be parallel to the horizontal centre crease. The circle shows how this fold is located. Crease firmly.

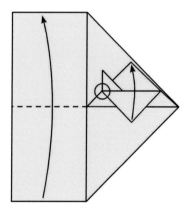

14. Unfold the fold made in step 13, then fold the whole plane in half upward.

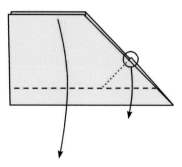

15. Remake fold 13, but this time extend the crease along the whole length of the plane to form the right-hand wing.

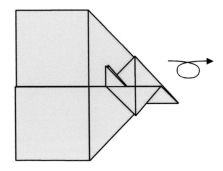

16. This is the result. Turn over sideways.

17. Fold the top layer in half downward, being careful to line up the edges of the wings.

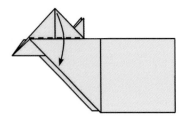

18. Fold the triangular flap downward as well. Crease firmly.

19. LIft the wings upward to match the profile shown.

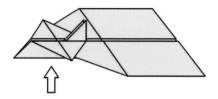

20. The Samurai can be launched
like a traditional glider.

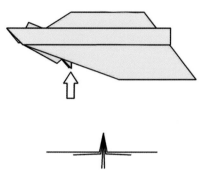

21. But it will also fly equally well, perhaps better,
the other way up.

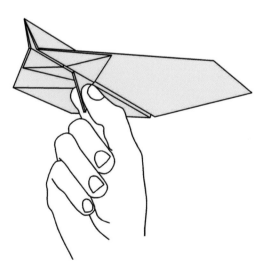

22. Hold by the horns and launch gently.

Designed by David Mitchell

The Fly

Paper plane designers have come up with many designs for planes that look like animals, insects, birds, or people. There are flying elephants, flying cranes, flying nuns, and flying Santas. This one is a flying fly!

The unique feature of this particular design is the elevators that masquerade as eyes. It shouldn't be possible to make a paper plane that flies so well with elevators on the leading edges of the wings. But it is! Proving once again that in paper plane design there are no hard and fast rules to follow. Anything goes, apparently. The trailing edges of the wings of the Fly are much the same shape as the trailing edges of the wings of Aerobat (page 74). You could try combining the two designs and equipping your Fly with elevators or wing-tip stabilizers, or both!

You will need a rectangle of ordinary paper. Begin with your paper arranged in the way shown in step 1.

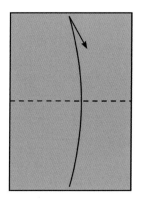

1. Fold in half upward, crease, then unfold.

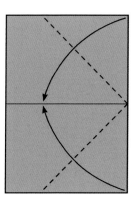

2. Fold both right-hand corners inward using the crease made in step 1 as a guide.

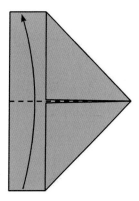

3. Fold in half upward.

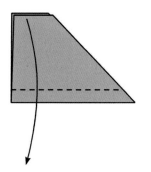

4. Create the first wing by folding the front layers downward.

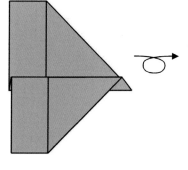

5. Turn over sideways.

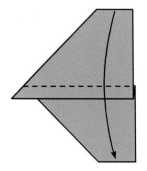

6. Create the second wing by folding the other layers downward to match.

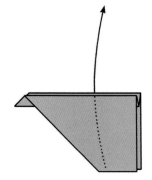

7. Open out folds 4 and 6 by pulling the rear wing upward as far as it will go.

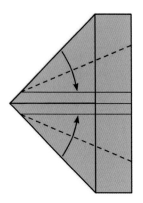

8. Narrow the wings using the folds made in steps 4 and 6 as guides.

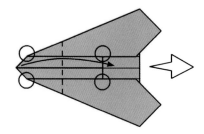

9. Fold the nose inward so that the points marked with circles end up lying on top of each other. The next picture is on a larger scale.

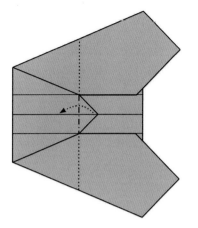

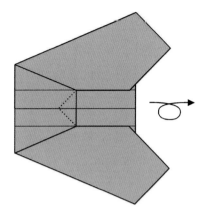

10. If you made fold 9 correctly you should now be able to tuck the tip of the top layer back underneath the loose flaps immediately behind it.

11. Turn over sideways.

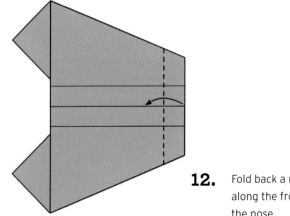

12. Fold back a narrow strip along the front edge of the nose.

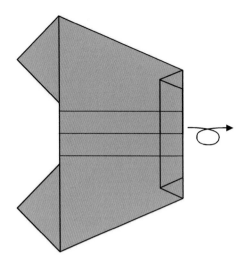

13. Turn over sideways again.

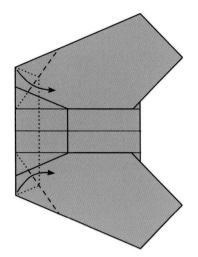

14. Fold the front corners of the wings inward to form the eyes. These folds begin where the wing/keel creases intersect the left hand edge. Fold over as much paper as you can. These folds do not affect the top layer of paper in the nose. Look at picture 15 to see what the result should look like.

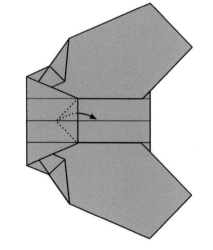

15. The folds made in step 14 should not lie flat. Allow them to stick up at about 45 degrees. Release the hidden triangular flap.

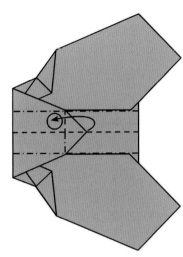

16. Remake the keel and wings to match the profile shown, using the existing creases. As you do this the small triangular flap released in step 14 will fold in half. Tuck this flap away sideways behind the loose layer beside it to lock the centre of the keel together.

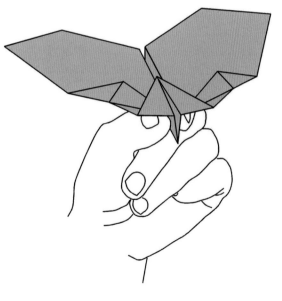

17. Launch gently in the normal way. If necessary adjust the angle of the eyes to improve the glide angle.

Spike

Designed by David Mitchell

Spike is the first design in this book to have a tailplane. All real aircraft have them, but pure origami paper planes seldom do. This is because tailplanes create drag at the back of the keel, which forces the nose upwards and causes the plane to stall. The design of Spike, though, is sufficiently front-heavy to compensate for this effect. In fact, Spike flies better with a tailplane than without.

The other unique feature of this design is the wonderful move that creates the shape of the nose and wings in steps 5 and 6. If you can't work out how to do this at first, persevere.

You will need a rectangle of ordinary paper.
Begin with your paper arranged in the way
shown in step 1.

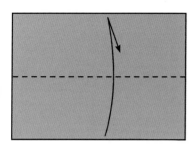

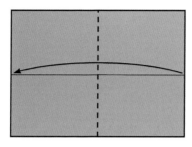

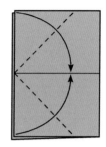

1. Fold in half upward, crease,
then unfold.

2. Fold in half sideways.

3. Fold both left-hand
corners of the front
layer inward, using the
horizontal crease as
a guide.

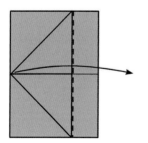

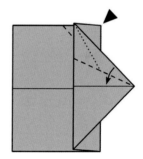

4. Fold the front layers across to the right so that
the crease forms along the vertical edges of
the triangular flaps.

5. Fold the front sloping edge onto the horizontal
crease. As you do this, push the top corner
inward and flatten the paper so that the result
looks like picture 6. Not easy, but not quite
impossible either.

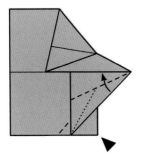
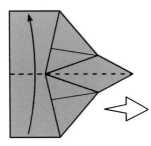
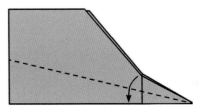

6. Repeat fold 5 on the bottom half of the design.

7. Fold in half upwards. The next picture is on a larger scale.

8. Fold the front layer of the nose in half downward. Extend the crease all the way to the tail.

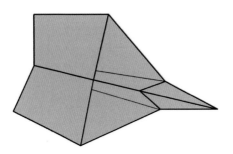

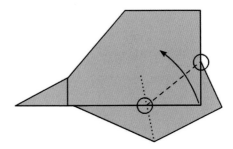

9. Turn over sideways.

10. Form the tailplane by folding the bottom right-hand corner of the top layer inward. Note how the left hand end of the crease is located by reference to the hidden edge of the paper. You can see this hidden edge by holding the design up to the light.

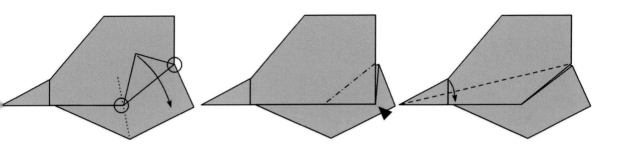

11. Open out the fold made in step 10.

12. Turn the tailplane inside out between the layers using the creases made in step 10.

13. Fold the second wing downward to match the first.

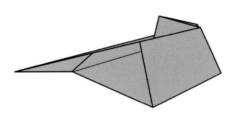

14. Lift the wings upward to match the profile shown.

15. Hold in the middle of the keel and launch in the normal way.

Blitzen

There is no other paper plane quite like Blitzen. Only Blitzen has twin fins instead of wing-tip stabilizers or a tailplane. They do the same job, but in a uniquely unusual way.

The way Blitzen is folded is also quite different from any other plane in this book. It is simple, elegant and effective. Paper plane designs are not often like this.

The original design that Blitzen was adapted from was folded from a square, but you can use a rectangle. The extra length gained by using a rectangle gives a better weight distribution and improved flight characteristics. Try the effect of creating fins underneath the wings rather than on top. Does Blitzen still fly?

You will need a rectangle of
ordinary paper.

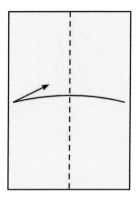

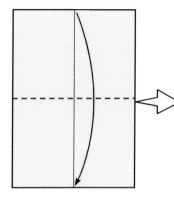

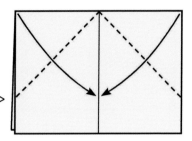

1. Begin with your paper
arranged in the way
shown in picture 1. Fold
in half sideways.

2. Fold in half downward.
The next picture is on a
larger scale.

3. Fold both top corners
inward using the crease
made in step 1 as a guide.

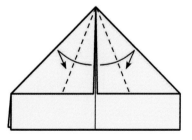

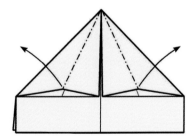

4. Fold the inside edges of the front flaps onto
the sloping edges, crease, then unfold.

5. Open out both flaps and squash them flat in the
position shown in step 6.

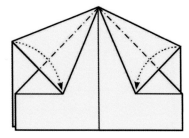 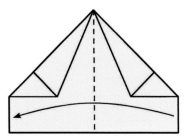 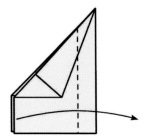

6. Fold both triangular flaps in half behind.

7. Fold in half from right to left.

8. Fold the front layers across to the right to form a wing. There are no exact location points for this fold.

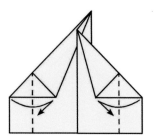

9. Fold just the front layers of each wingtip inward to form stabilizers, crease, then unfold.

10. Turn over sideways.

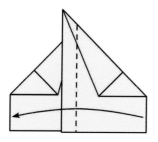  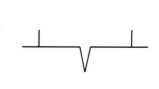

11. Fold the second wing across to the left to match the first.

12. Open out the wings and stabilizers to match the profile shown.

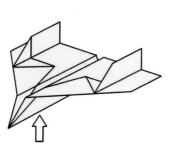 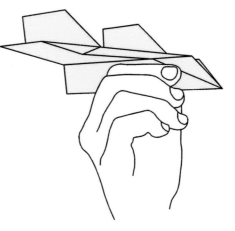

13. Blitzen is finished.

14. Hold and launch in the normal way. Blitzen doesn't just look good, it flies well too!

Art Deco Wing

One of the most essential elements in paper plane design is the keel. True or false? Well, false, actually. The Art Deco Wing is inanimate proof that whatever rules there are in paper plane design can be broken. The Art Deco Wing is just that, a wing, or perhaps two wings linked together. The point is that the wing lies completely flat. Whatever you do, don't put a crease between them to create a keel! The design works best from lightweight paper. Origami paper is ideal.

    Step 18 shows how the wing is launched. You will get a longer flight if you hold the Art Deco Wing as high as possible above your head. The designer also suggests holding the wing by the nose and throwing it straight up into the air. In fact virtually any way that you can get some extra height into the launch will help. Jumping, or standing on a chair, perhaps? Try making tiny adjustments to the stabilizers to achieve optimum performance.

You will need a square of ordinary paper. Begin with your paper arranged in the way shown in step 1.

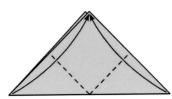

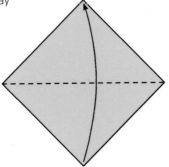

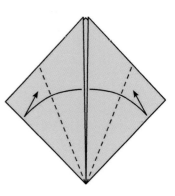

1. Fold in half upward.

2. Fold both bottom corners up to the top point.

3. Fold each of the front flaps in half outward, crease, then unfold.

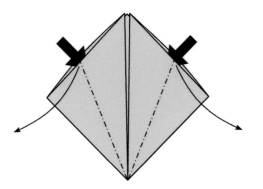

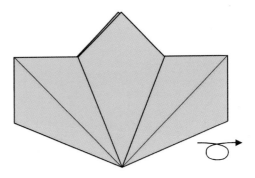

4. Put a finger inside each pocket, open them out, then squash them flat in turn. Picture 5 shows what the result should look like.

5. Turn over sideways.

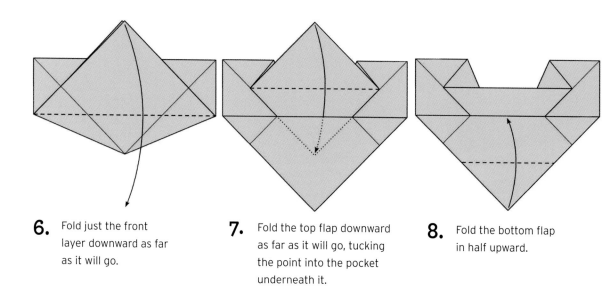

6. Fold just the front layer downward as far as it will go.

7. Fold the top flap downward as far as it will go, tucking the point into the pocket underneath it.

8. Fold the bottom flap in half upward.

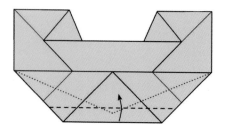

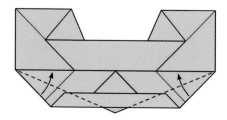

9. Fold the bottom flap upward again. The dotted line shows the outline of the layers underneath. The point of these hidden layers should become visible once the fold has been made.

10. Pull out the hidden flaps.

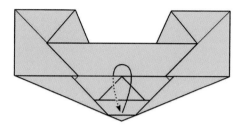

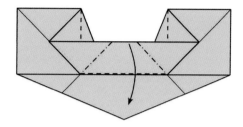

11. Turn the corners inside out between the other layers using the existing creases.

12. Fold the middle flap downward over the layers that lie below it. Make the crease as long as you can and then flatten the rest of the paper so that the result looks like step 13.

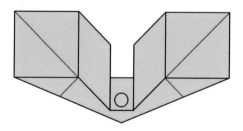

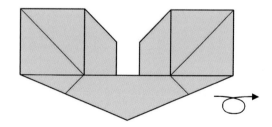

13. Tuck the flap marked with a circle into the pocket that lies behind it.

14. Turn over sideways.

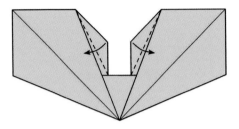 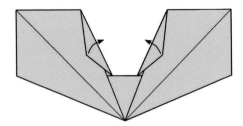

15. Create stabilizers by folding the central flaps outward as far as the overlying layers will permit.

16. Lift the stabilizers up at right angles.

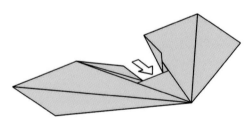 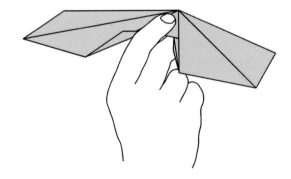

17. The finished Art Deco Wing should look like this.

18. Hold between the wings and launch with a gentle push forward.

Supersonic

Unlike real aircraft, paper planes do not have huge engines to provide them with a continuous supply of forward thrust. The only thrust a paper plane gets is the thrust you give it when you launch it. It is quite literally downhill from there on in. Supersonic is no exception to this rule, but it flies faster, higher, and farther because the launch is powered by a rubber band, which can provide more thrust more quickly than your muscles can.

Choosing the right rubber band is the crucial thing. Ideally you want one that is fairly long and fairly thin. The newer it is (the less times it has been stretched already) the better.

You will need a rectangle of ordinary paper,
a staple and an elastic band. Begin with your
paper arranged in the way shown in step 1.

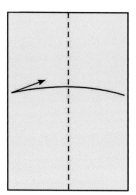

1. Fold in half sideways, crease, then unfold.

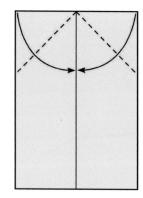

2. Fold both the top corners inward, using the crease made in step 1 as a guide.

3. Fold the top point downward so that the new crease forms just below the bottom edges of the triangular flaps.

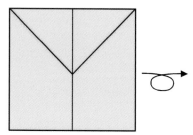

4. Turn over sideways.

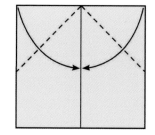

5. Repeat step 2 on the new top corners.

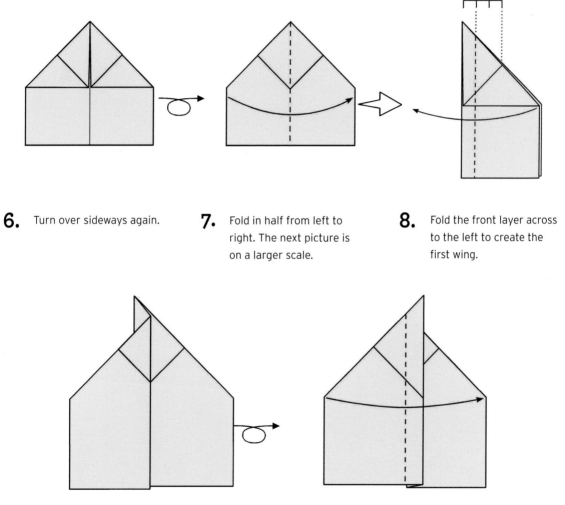

6. Turn over sideways again.

7. Fold in half from left to right. The next picture is on a larger scale.

8. Fold the front layer across to the left to create the first wing.

9. Turn over sideways.

10. Fold the other wing across to match.

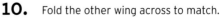

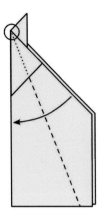

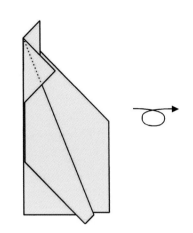

11. Fold the sloping edge of the front wing across to lie along the left-hand edge. Look at step 12 to see what the result should look like. You should only be folding the layers of the wing itself and not the pocket it runs into at the top. Make sure that the crease runs all the way to the point marked with a circle. You will find it easier to do this if you open up the pocket slightly while you make the fold.

12. Turn over sideways.

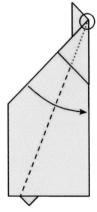

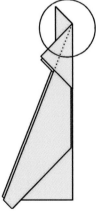

13. Repeat step 11 on the other wing.

14. Follow the instructions in the enlargements t turn the nose into a hook.

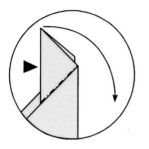

15. Turn the tip of the nose inside out between the layers of the keel.

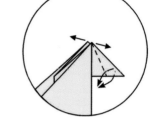

16. Open the nose and turn the tip of the triangular point inside out outside the other layers, to form the hook.

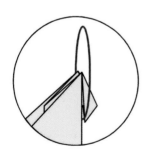

17. Make sure there is a small gap between the hook and the underside of the keel into which a thin rubber band can be slipped without sticking.

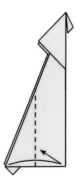

18. Fold the front wing in half sideways, crease, then unfold.

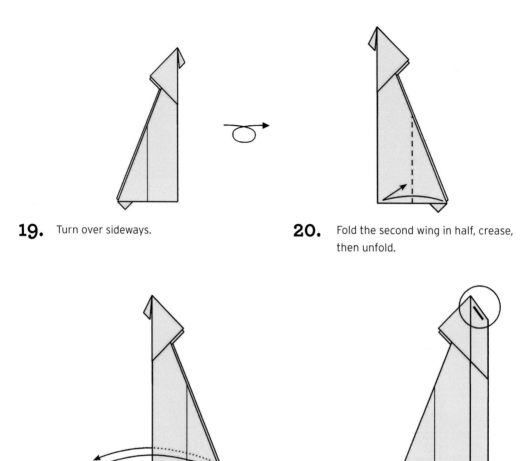

19. Turn over sideways.

20. Fold the second wing in half, crease, then unfold.

21. Open both wings out to the left.

22. Put a staple through the nose to hold all the layers together.

23. Arrange the wings and wingtip stabilizers to match the profile shown.

24. Attach a thin elastic band to the hook and launch in the way shown in step 25. Because of the rubber band-powered boost it is best to launch Supersonic outdoors in a wide open space. Try to choose a calm, almost windless day.

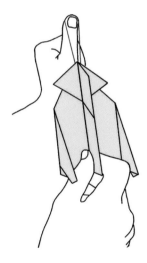

25. To launch Supersonic, loop the band onto the tip of your thumb, hold the back of the keel in your other hand, pull back to tension the band, then release. Experiment to find the launch angle and speed that will produce the longest flight.

Designed by Robin Glynn

Glynn's Glider

The finished version of Glynn's Glider looks very little different from the Basic Glider explained at the beginning of this book. You will need a very large room. Appearances, though, can be deceptive. The secret of this quite wonderful design lies in the clever way the weight has been distributed between the wings, keel and nose to create a glider that will fly the maximum distance in a straight line.

This is not just theoretical. On September 19, 1977, at the Yorkshire Air Museum in England a version of Glynn's Glider essentially similar to the one explained here set the world distance record for a pure origami plane (as defined by the *Guinness Book of Records* rules), flying a straight line distance of 94ft or 28.7m. This may not sound far, but just try to beat it!

You will need a rectangle of ordinary paper. Begin with your paper arranged in the way shown in step 1.

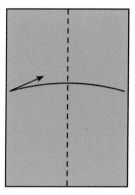

1. Fold in half sideways, crease, then unfold.

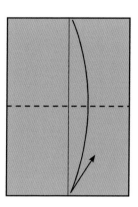

2. Fold in half downward, crease, then unfold.

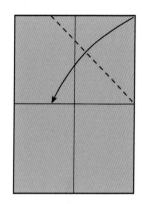

3. Fold the top right-hand corner inward, using the crease made in step 2 as a guide.

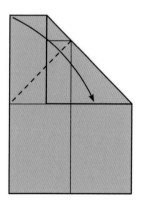

4. Fold the top left hand corner inward in a similar way.

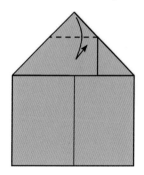

5. Fold the top downward along the line of the hidden edge of the inside layer, crease, then unfold. You can feel where the hidden edge is as soon as you begin to make the fold. Be as accurate as you can.

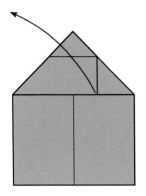

6. Open out the fold made in step 4.

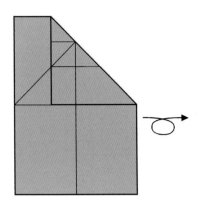

7. Turn over sideways.

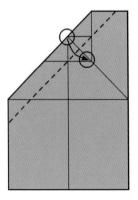

8. Fold the sloping edge inward as shown, using the points marked with circles to locate the fold accurately. Allow the hidden flap to flip into sight as you make the fold. The crease is only made in one layer of paper.

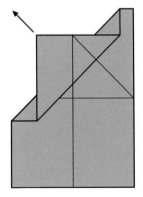

9. Pull the top left-hand corner back into place.

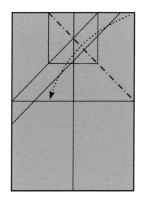

10. Fold the top right-hand out of sight using the crease made in step 4.

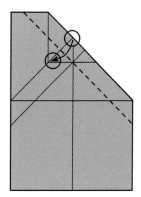

11. Repeat step 6 on the right-hand side of the paper.

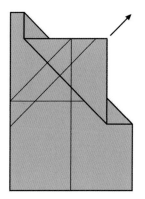

12. Pull the top right-hand corner back into place.

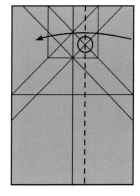

13. Fold the right-hand edge across to the left to begin to form the keel. Use the intersection of the two diagonal creases (marked with a circle) to locate this fold.

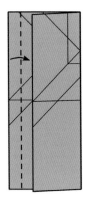

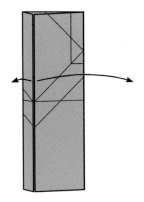

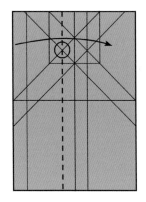

14. Fold the left-hand edge inward, using the original right-hand edge of the paper as a guide.

15. Undo the folds made in steps 13 and 14.

16. Repeat fold 13 in the opposite direction.

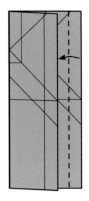

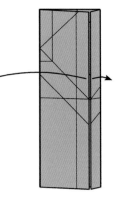

17. Then repeat step 14 as well.

18. Undo the folds made in steps 16 and 17.

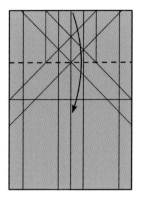 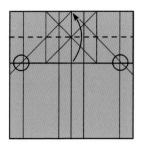 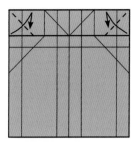

19. Fold the top downward, using the line of the horizontal crease made in step 6 as a guide.

20. Note how the creases line up at the points marked with circles. Fold the front flap upwards again.

21. Fold the corners of the top flap inward as shown, crease, then unfold.

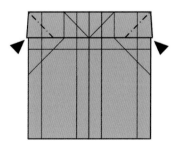 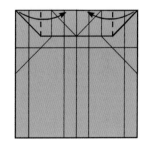

22. Turn the corners inside out using the creases made in step 21.

23. Fold the loose flaps inward as shown.

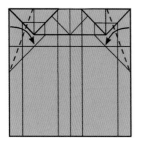

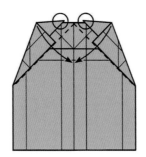

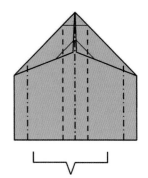

24. Fold both the top corners inward, using the sloping creases made in steps 3 and 4 as guides.

25. Fold both the top corners inward again using the creases made in steps 3 and 4 (which have to be remade through some new layers.) As you do this tuck the triangular flaps marked with circles into the pocket that lies underneath them.

26. Remake the creases forming the keel, wings and wingtip stabilizers through all the layers to match the profile shown.

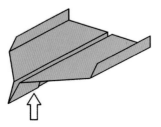

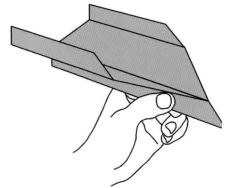

27. Glynn's Glider is finished.

28. You will find that you can launch this glider fairly fast in an upward direction. In still conditions it will fly a very long way indeed.

Jinx

Jinx is a sophisticated origami version of the Starfighter TFB-5, which comes complete with tailplane and afterburners. It not only looks good but it flies well too, in the correct position, with the fuselage above the wings. Jinx may not be the ultimate paper plane, but it comes very, very close.

If you have long fingernails you can launch Jinx in the way shown in picture 35. If you don't, try launching it by holding the nose. The designer also suggests that another good launch method (if you have enough ceiling height) is to grip the front of the left wing next to the fuselage with the bottom of the model facing you and to launch straight up. Jinx will first execute a loop and then settle into a gentle glide at a higher altitude than with a regular launch. Try making delicate adjustments to the elevators to improve the flight characteristics.

You will need a square of lightweight paper. Begin
with your paper arranged in the way shown in step 1.

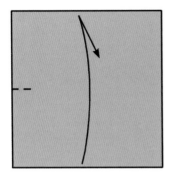

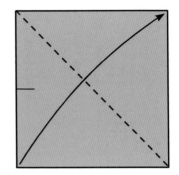

1. Fold in half upward, pinch to mark the centre of
the left-hand edge, then unfold.

2. Fold in half diagonally.

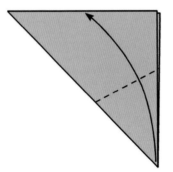

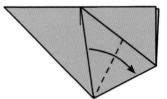

3. Fold the bottom point onto the top edge, using
the pinch mark made in step 1 to locate the fold.

4. Fold the triangular flap in half.

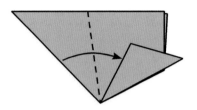

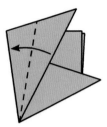

5. Fold the sloping left-hand edge inward, using the edge of the front flap as a guide.

6. Fold the left-hand front flap in half.

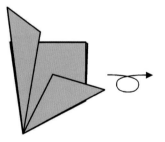

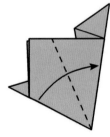

7. Turn over sideways.

8. Fold in half again through all layers.

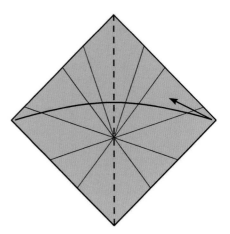

9. Open out completely by undoing all the folds (and the sideways turnover) in sequence back to the beginning.

10. Arrange the paper like this, and check you can remake fold 2 without reversing the direction of the existing crease. (If you would have to reverse the direction of the crease, you need to turn your paper over sideways.)

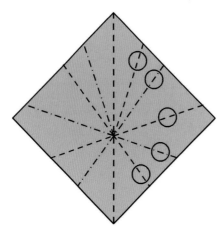

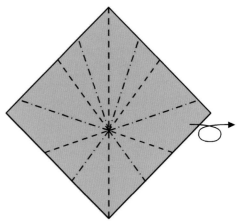

11. This picture shows the direction of all the creases. You need to reverse the direction of the five creases on the right-hand side (all marked with circles). Make sure you don't reverse any of the ones on the left!

12. This is the result. Check that each alternate crease is now made in a different direction through the paper. When you are sure this is so, turn over sideways.

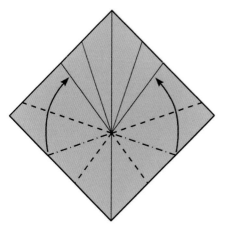

13. Begin to collapse the design by making the two folds shown. The paper will not lie flat when you have done this.

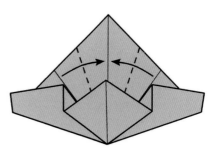

14. Complete the collapse by making two further folds like this. The paper will now lie flat again. The next picture is on a slightly larger scale.

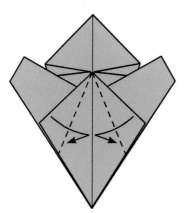

15. This is the result. You can see Jinx beginning to take shape. Fold the top edges of the front flap inward using the vertical centre crease as a guide, crease, then unfold.

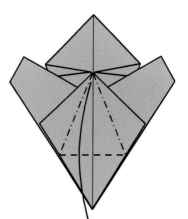

16. Fold the tip of the front flap downward and flatten it in the new position by reversing the creases made in step 15. You will have to make two new creases in the underlying layers as well. Look at step 17 to see what the result should look like.

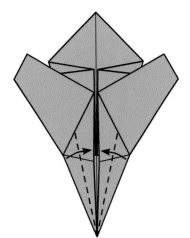

17. Thin the nose from both sides.

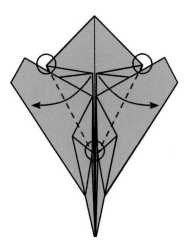

18. Fold the front layers outward to both sides as shown. The location points are marked with circles.

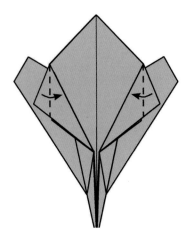

19. Fold the tips of both the front triangular flaps inward.

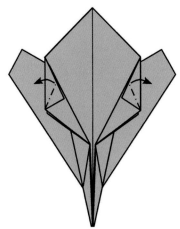

20. Lift and squash these flaps to create afterburners.

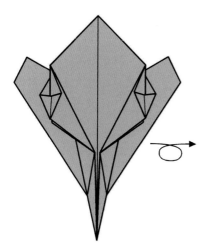

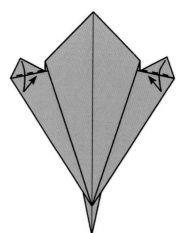

21. Turn over sideways.

22. Fold the single-layer triangular flaps downward over the back edges of the wings to form elevators, crease, then unfold.

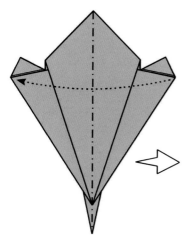

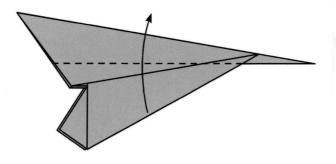

23. Fold in half sideways so that the undersides of the wings are in contact and rotate to align to step 22. The next picture is on a larger scale.

24. The wing creases continue the line of the underside of the nose backward to the tail. Fold the first wing upward like this.

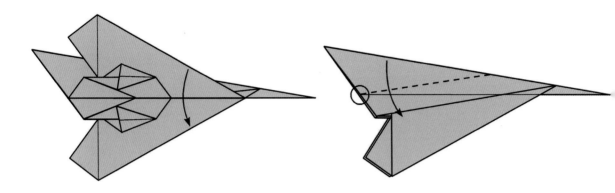

25. Fold the wing downward again.

26. Fold the tail downward. The crease should be made parallel to the folded edge below it.

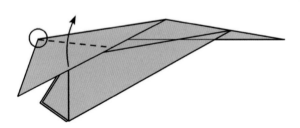

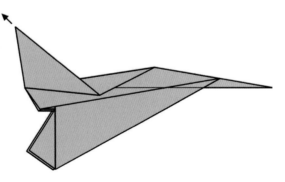

27. Fold the tip of the tail upward again. The result should look like step 28.

28. Pull the tip of the tail upward to undo the last two folds.

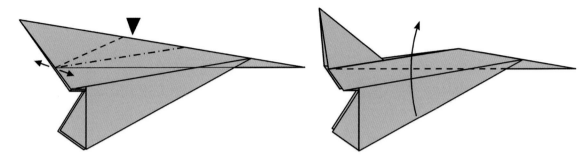

29. Open the back layers and zigzag the tail into position between them using the creases made in steps 26 and 27.

30. Fold the wing back up again.

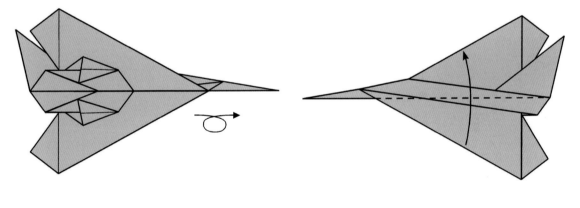

31. Turn over sideways.

32. Fold the second wing upwards to match the first.

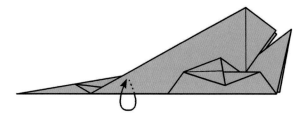

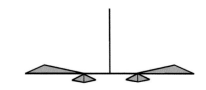

33. There are two small flaps inside the front of the fuselage. Pull the back one down then tuck it up inside the pocket in front of the other one. This will seal the front of the fuselage.

34. Lower the wings, make the afterburners three-dimensional, and raise the elevators slightly to match the profile shown.

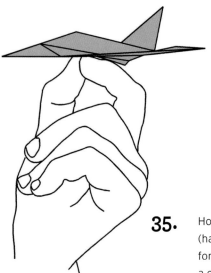

35. Hold by the central fin inside the fuselage (having long nails helps!) and launch gently forwards. Jinx flies surprisingly well for such a complex paper plane.

Dictionary of Symbols

The edges of the paper are shown as solid lines.

A folding instruction consists of a movement arrow and a fold-line. The movement arrow shows the direction in which the fold is made. The fold-line shows where the new crease will form. A combination of a solid movement arrow and a dotted fold-line means the fold is made in front of the paper.

This is the result of following the folding instruction shown above. Edges which lie exactly on top of each other as the result of a fold are normally shown slightly offset on the after diagram.

A movement arrow without a fold-line means unfold in the direction indicated.

This is the result of following the unfold instruction shown above. Creases you have already made are shown by thin lines.

This version of the movement arrow means fold, crease, then unfold.

A combination of a dotted movement arrow and a dashed and dotted fold-line means the fold is made behind the paper.

A diagram of this kind tells you to swing the flap out of sight underneath the paper by reversing the direction of the existing crease.

This is the result of following the above instruction. Dotted lines are sometimes used to show the edges of hidden flaps.

This symbol shows how the adjacent edge can be seen as divided into a number of equal sections to help you locate a fold.

A combination of the two types of fold-line shows that the creases you have made run in different directions through the paper.

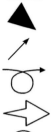

This symbol tells you to apply gentle pressure to the paper in the direction the arrowhead is pointing.

This symbol tells you to move part of the paper in the direction of the arrow.

The turnover symbol tells you to turn the paper over sideways before making the next fold.

The enlargement arrow tells you that the next diagram has been drawn to a larger scale.

A circle is used to draw attention to some particular part of a picture that you need to look at carefully. Circles are also used as the boundaries of enlarged drawings where only part of the paper is shown.

Author's Acknowledgments

I am indebted to the many paper plane enthusiasts whose ideas, experience, and sense of fun have contributed to the creation of this book. We all stand upon each others' shoulders.

My particular thanks are due to Nick Robinson, Max Hulme, Michael La Fosse. Larry Hart, Yoshihide Momotani, Robin Glynn and Marvin Goody for lending me their marvellous designs.

Going further with paperfolding

If you have enjoyed folding and flying the designs in this book you can learn more about paper planes, and origami in general, by visiting the author's website www.origamiheaven.com

For those who want to take things further still, there are specialist origami clubs in many countries which arrange meetings and publish magazines and collections of new designs, including new and innovative designs for paper planes. The two main English speaking are the British Origami Society and Origami USA, both of which are not-for-profit organisations run entirely by volunteers. Both have a worldwide membership base.

Origami USA can be contacted through www.origami-usa.org

The British Origami Society can be contacted through www.britishorigami.org.uk